EMBRACING LIFE AS IT IS

ALSO BY ALAN GETTIS, PHD

Seven Times Down, Eight Times Up:
Landing on Your Feet in an Upside Down World —
Second Edition Revised and Expanded

The Happiness Solution:
Finding Joy and Meaning in an Upside Down World

It's All Part of the Dance:
Finding Happiness in an Upside Down World

In the Beak of a Duck

EMBRACING LIFE AS IT IS

LESSONS FROM WABI-SABI, HAIKU, AND ZEN

ALAN GETTIS, PHD
CARL GENJO BACHMANN

PHOTOGRAPHY BY CYNDI GOETCHEUS SARFAN

GOODMAN BECK PUBLISHING

Goodman Beck Publishing
PO Box 253
Norwood, NJ 07648
goodmanbeck.com

ISBN 978-1-936636-01-3

Library of Congress Control Number: 2018957785

Printed in the United States of America

This book has been printed using recycled, acid-free paper.

10 9 8 7 6 5 4 3 2 1

First Edition

ALAN GETTIS

I dedicate this book to the light of my life, my granddaughter, Juliana.

CARL GENJO BACHMANN

This book is dedicated to my dear teacher, Roshi Robert Kennedy.

CYNDI GOETCHEUS SARFAN

I dedicate this book to all my family members whose love, forgiveness, and support helped me learn to embrace my own messy and imperfect life, and who have guided me steadfastly on my journey toward self-acceptance.

CONTENTS

INTRODUCTION

In haiku, we pay attention to the moment without embellishment. We embrace the moment as it is, not how we would like it to be. Just this, right here, right now.

Wabi-sabi is paying attention to and appreciating this object or this person at this time, as is, also without embellishment. It's valuing imperfection, impermanence, and the natural devolving of everything born or made. Just this, right here, right now, as is.

Zen also teaches us to pay attention. The past is gone. The future is unknown. The only thing we have is this present moment. Meditation helps us to mindfully attend to this moment, just this breath, right here and right now. We learn to be where we are, completely.

Our premise is that wabi-sabi, haiku, and Zen all provide important lessons in many things, including selflessness, acceptance, nondiscrimination, compassion, self-compassion, and impermanence.

We hope you enjoy this book and that it guides you to live fully in the present moment.

In gratitude,
Alan Gettis
Sensei Carl Genjo Bachmann

WABI-SABI

There is a Zen story usually referred to as "No Water, No Moon." It is about the nun Chiyono, who after many years of study and practice became enlightened because of a beautiful moon reflected in the pail of water she was carrying. She wrote the following poem:

> In this way and that I tried to save the old pail
> Since the bamboo strip was weakening and about to break
> Until at last the bottom fell out.
> No more water in the pail!
> No more moon in the water!

Another translation has the opening line of the poem as: "With this and that I tried to keep the bucket together." Yes, we can use all our studies, wealth, skills, technical knowledge, and resources to try and keep the bucket together, but the bottom falls out again and again. In Zen and wabi-sabi, there is no perfect bucket. How wonderful for Chiyono the nun that the bottom fell out. She awoke.

> A pointed-roof hut in the shade of the clouds
> A broken-legged pot on a pile of dry leaves
> A strainer with holes too big to strain rice
> And a cracked grating bowl for grating fresh ginger.[1]

Wabi-sabi is the appreciation of things impermanent, imperfect, and incomplete. In wabi-sabi we find value, beauty, and interest in unlikely places, and an acceptance and appreciation of life as it is rather than life as we wish it would be. We discover the beauty of objects that are decomposing, and we realize we are no less valuable, loveable, or beautiful as a result of our own decomposition. Wabi-sabi is the stone with moss. It's the faded, dog-eared book. It is about objects, people, you and me, all worn through use and the passage of time.

Pared down to is barest essence, wabi-sabi is the Japanese art of finding beauty in and accepting the natural cycle of growth, decay, and death. It's simple, slow, and uncluttered — and it reveres authenticity above all. The esteemed architect Tadao Ando points out that wabi-sabi celebrates cracks and crevices and all the other marks that time, weather, and loving use leave behind. It reminds us that we are all but transient beings on this planet — that our bodies as well as the material world around us are in the process of returning to the dust from which we came. Through wabi-sabi we learn to embrace liver spots, rust, and frayed edges, and the march of time they represent.[2]

Wabi-sabi objects all have a story. We and our possessions have histories that give us character and a one-of-a-kind essence. We have all evolved, and we are all devolving. We are marked by life as it presses upon us. Now, in my (Gettis) seventies, I grow shorter and more asymmetrical, and many scars and markings are part of the story of my life. Wabi-sabi instructs me in the beauty and wisdom of aging and vulnerability. It helps me appreciate the adage, "The older the fiddler, the sweeter the tune."

The word *utopia*, which means the perfect place, is of Greek origin. Its literal translation is: U = no, and topia = place. So as it turns out, the perfect place is no place. And similarly, the perfect person is no person. We need not only to accept our imperfections, but to honor them. Imperfection is our birthright. It is in our nature, our genes, our biochemistry, and our psyches, somas, and souls.

Ring the bells that still can ring.
Forget your perfect offering.
There is a crack, a crack in everything.
That's how the light gets in.
— Leonard Cohen

Madison Avenue bombards us with ideas such as, "Buy this perfect product, get that perfect life."[3] Just about every commercial suggests there is something wrong with us. Anti-aging products permeate the marketplace. Our "as is" condition is evidently unacceptable. We believe if we can stop aging and wear new designer clothing and drive the latest unscathed cars, we'll be happy. There is a stampede for the newest, slickest, and perfect this or perfect that.

Wabi-sabi is the antithesis of that. It is about life without pretense, without fairytale endings, without immortality, without perfection. Wabi-sabi is about life as it is. It encompasses the:

imperfect

impermanent

incomplete

irregular

rustic

earthy

unpretentious

simple

odd

misshapen

understated

coarse

raw

unrefined

unassuming

modest

weathered

mortal

unpolished

ephemeral

ambiguous

one-of-a-kind

subtle

fallible

cracked

rusted

faced

worn

crude

nooks and crannies

crevices

patina of age

solitude

decomposition

character

authenticity

transient

idiosyncratic

textured

flawed

frayed

passage of time

humility

tenderness

asymmetry

natural

erosion

unpredictable

unusual

intimate

contradictory

material poverty

spiritual richness

Leonard Koren, the author of a wonderful book called *Wabi-Sabi for Artists, Designers, Poets & Philosophers,* considers wabi-sabi to be an anti-aesthetic that was the offspring of beat, punk, and grunge. Wabi-sabi reflected the spiritual and metaphysical simplicity and acceptance of life that was emphasized in Taoism and Chinese Zen Buddhism. Almost like an "aha" moment or a haiku moment, wabi-sabi stirs us to see the organic, natural, earthy process of aging. Speaking of wabi-sabi objects, Koren states:

> They are made of materials that are visibly vulnerable to the effects of weathering and human treatment. They record the sun, wind, rain, heat, and cold in a language of discoloration, rust, tarnish, stain, warping, shrinking, shriveling, and cracking. Their nicks, chips, bruises, scars, dents, peeling, and other forms of attrition are a testament to histories of use and misuse. Though things wabi-sabi may be on the point of dematerialization (or materialization) — extremely faint, fragile, or desiccated — they still possess an undiminished poise and strength of character.[4]

Zen points to sunyata, or the suchness of things, i.e., isness. Wabi-sabi is both isness and as-isness. It is things and people and events as they are, as is. If we were at a garage sale or a flea market or an antique store, we would find items and either we or the sellers would point out the flaws and imperfections. The seller would then tell us that we are buying it in that condition — as is. That is what life is about: as is. And that is what wabi-sabi is about — the as-isness.

I've (Gettis) defined grace as when we stop wrestling with Mother Nature, Father Time, and cosmic indifference. I've often thought that I could define happiness and peace of mind the same way. And we may really appreciate wabi-sabi when we stop wrestling with Mother Nature, Father Time, and cosmic indifference.

Wabi-sabi is not epic. It is neither a spectacle, spectacular, or monumental. It is more of a small independent film that's a character study, versus a big studio, blockbuster action film.

"The closer things get to nonexistence, the more exquisite and evocative they become. Consequently, to experience wabi-sabi means you have to slow down, be patient, and look very closely."[5]

Despite wabi-sabi being an aesthetic of decomposition, and despite it offering us no escape from mortality, illness, old age, and death, wabi-sabi points to life being full of purpose, meaning, and joy. There is no grief without love. There is no sadness without happiness. Appreciating wabi-sabi increases our gratitude and compassion for our short and imperfect lives. Richard R. Powell frames it this way:

> The complete term wabi-sabi describes a way of life practiced by those who notice and appreciate the significant moments of each day, live fully in each change of season, and connect with nature and those around them in meaningful and gentle ways.[6]

Wabi comes from the root *wa*, which connotes harmony, balance, and being in tune with nature. Sabi refers to the natural effects of the passage of time. It is understanding that beauty, fame, power, and life itself fade and are fleeting.[7]

Can we live our lives with dignity and grace as the inevitability of aging and its effects naturally manifest themselves? We are like the oxidized bronze Buddha, the deteriorating red barn, the 1953 DesSoto abandoned near the creek....

Tadao Ando points out that wabi-sabi is a mindset: living modestly, being satisfied with life as it is, and living in the moment. He addresses the thought that wabi-sabi is un-American when he states, "I believe there exists in all of us a longing for something deeper than the whitest teeth, sparkling floors, and eight cylinders. What if we could learn to be content with our lives, exactly as they are today?"[8]

We know that all forms ruin sooner or later, and that we cannot stop or control this relentless and universal truth. Koren says, "Even things that have all the earmarks of substance — things that are hard, inert, solid — present nothing more than the *illusion* of permanence. We may wear blinders, use ruses to forget, ignore, or pretend otherwise — but all comes to nothing in the end."

He continues, "The planets and stars, and even intangible things like reputation, family heritage, historical memory, scientific theorems, mathematical proofs, great art and literature (even in digital form) — all eventually fade into oblivion and nonexistence."[9]

Wabi-sabi is bittersweet. We must consider our own decay and ultimate mortality, yet find the beauty and peace-of-mind in this natural and timeless wisdom. Wabi-sabi doesn't judge, criticize, analyze, obsess, or cling. It allows us and things to be imperfect, which helps us not to continually dwell on things that don't deserve our attention.

Our lives are characterized by the Japanese expression *Seven Times Down, Eight Times Up*. There will always be stumbles, falls, challenges, wrinkles, and problems as we and objects "rust out," so to speak. Accepting this is loving ourselves unconditionally. We appreciate and are grateful for life as it really is, rather than life as we would like it to be.

It is not about fantasy. By embracing the Zen truth that everything changes (you can't step into the same river twice), wabi-sabi enables us to appreciate the ephemeral nature of things and helps us to achieve peace of mind as we experience the imperfections that come along with life as part of the bargain.

Koren believes, "Wabi-sabi can, in its fullest expression, be a way of life."[10] I fully agree with this premise. Our thinking, attitudes, feelings, and behaviors change as we grow into wabi-sabi mind. There is no reason to give ourselves a hard time psychologically if we are honoring aging and our unique quirks and oddities. Wabi-sabi celebrates the passage of time and the natural uniqueness of you and me and everything.[11] We and life and our own world are perfectly imperfect.

HAIKU

I think haiku
is the most beautiful
form of poetry I know.
—John Lennon
(John Lennon Museum, Japan)

The sound of rain needs no translation.
—Alan Watts

HAIKU: AN INTRODUCTION

Ah, the haiku moment. Just this! Right here, right now. The experience of seeing and feeling deeply *Just This*, as if for the first time. Many believe that a haiku is any poem of three lines that contains seventeen syllables. That is not usually the case. Haiku may well be "literature's most subtle art form," sophisticated, parsimonious, and conveying a moment of experiential truth.

Matsuo Basho, perhaps the greatest haiku poet of Japan, introduced the form in the middle of the seventeenth century. It differed markedly from other poetic forms. The language used was ordinary. It was pedestrian rather than pedantic. Typical poetic devices such as rhyming, simile, personification, metaphor, and hyperbole were not used.

Originally, Japanese haiku were three lines, with five syllables in the first line, seven syllables in the middle line, and five syllables in the third line. The classic haiku poets of Japan more often than not stuck to this 5-7-5 format. As it turns out, the Japanese syllable is different than the English syllable, making Japanese haiku sound more concise than the English haiku containing seventeen syllables. Therefore, many English-speaking haiku poets use fewer than seventeen syllables. Even Japanese-speaking poets have written thousands of haiku containing fewer syllables or more syllables. One of the most important Japanese haiku poets, Shiki, advised, "Break rules if necessary."[2]

Basho said, "Haiku is simply what is happening in this place, at this time. It is eternal Now. There is no other time than this moment. The past is no more. The future is not yet. Deep in the mountains, the great temple bell is struck. You hear it reverberating in the morning air, and all thoughts disappear from your mind. There is nothing that is you; there is nothing that is not you. There is only the sound of the bell...."[3]

Western poetry may use poetic devices such as alliteration, metaphor, onomatopeia, personification, rhyme, simile, and hyperbole. Let's compare a Western poet's poem about a frog with the most referenced haiku of all time, by Basho, and also about a frog.

> "How Many?"
> How many frogs does it take
> dying in the dust
> croaking in the crusted puddles?
> How many frog legs limping lamely?
> Oh, how true...
> it ain't easy being green...
> when life has gone all obscene.
> How many frogs must fall
> before we all recall
> the heart of life,
> and the
> miracle
> of it all?
> —Susan Henderson[4]

In contrast is the aforementioned haiku of Basho (translated by Alan Watts).

> The old pond —
> a frog jumps in.
> Plop![5]

So, we have two poets looking at a frog, one with the analytical eyes of the West, and the other with the spirit of Zen. Basho simply points to something and leaves it undisturbed. Just this, right here, right now. This moment, this truth, this pond, this frog, this splash.

Let's look at another example contrasting a Western poem with a haiku, both of which deal with the death of a cat. First, we have Christina Georgina Rossetti. Only the first two stanzas will be cited here:

"On the Death of a Cat"

Who shall tell the lady's grief
When her cat was past relief?
Who shall number the hot tears
Shed o'er her, belov'd for years?
Who shall say the dark dismay
Which her dying caused that day?

Come, ye muses, one and all,
Come obedient to my call;
Come and mourn with tuneful breath
Each one for a separate death,
And, while you in numbers sigh,
I will sing her elegy.[6]

Let's compare the above poem with that of haiku poet Michael McClintock:

dead cat...
open-mouthed
to the pouring rain[7]

Rossetti's poem employs rhyming, sentimentality, and asks numerous rhetorical questions. McClintock's haiku is a profound, yet disturbing, blunt moment of what is—not of what he would like to see, but of the truth of that moment. No proselytizing, no telling you how to feel, no judgment, no embellishment, nothing extra. A good haiku is lean, never containing anything extra or unnecessary.

Haiku see things in their suchness without comment. The Japanese call this view of the world *sono-mama*, which means, "Just as it is," or "Just so." This state of mind is "mushin,"[8] or literally, the state of no-mind. No ego, no explanations or interpretations. Nothing but the thusness of the haiku moment. Haiku is not simply a poetic form, but rather a way of experiencing life by intensifying perception.

> pier sunset
> in old wooden baskets
> crabs crawl on crabs
> — Alan Gettis

Haiku may lead to an aha moment, an epiphany, an awakening, or a similar experience in which you have a sudden awareness of the truth of the moment, or of a truth about life.

Isness. Suchness. "Only THIS—capital THIS—is. Anything and everything that appears to us as an individual entity or phenomenon, whether it be a planet or an atom, a mouse or a man, is but a temporary manifestation of THIS in form.... THIS is all the while only and always *this* frog, *this* pond, *this* plop!, *this* man, *this* woman, *this* child, *this* sun and rain and rainbow, the birth of *this* owl, the death of *this* mouse, *this* rotting corpse by the roadside, *this* lively maggot emerging, *this* cuckoo calling now...."[9]

A SUGGESTION ON READING HAIKU

Take your time. Consider reading them twice. You may enjoy reading them aloud. With each haiku, visualize the image. Each haiku is like a cup of tea. Slow down, relax, and take it in.

Many of the haiku selected for this book were chosen for their wabi-sabi flavor. The wabi-sabi section of this book preceded the haiku section by design. We believe you may resonate with and appreciate the haiku more because you read the wabi-sabi section first.

a bitter morning:
sparrows sitting together
without any necks
—J.W. Hackett[10]

What's gone is already gone
and what hasn't come needs no thought
right now i'm writing a right-now line
plums are ripe and gardenias in bloom[11]

HAIKU FROM THE JAPANESE MASTERS

that is good, this too is good—
New Year's Day
in my old age
—Royto

the old man
hoeing the field,
has his hat on crooked
—Kito

the scarecrow in the distance;
it walked with me
as I walked
—Sanin

a willow
and two or three cows
waiting for the boat
—Shiki

bent over by the rain,
the ears of barley
make it a narrow path
— Joso

along this road
goes no one,
this autumn eve
— Basho

in the abandoned boat,
the hail
bounces about
— Shiki

the thief
left it behind —
the moon at the window
— Ryokan

CONTEMPORARY HAIKU

blending coolness
with Billie Holiday
the blue ceiling fan
— Michael McClintock

twisting inland,
the sea fog takes a while
in the apple trees
— Michael McClintock

warm river—
up to our necks
in sunset
—Ruth Yarrow

the empty mountain house
falling into
itself

— Adele Kenny

long after
the leaping buck — the quiver
of the fence post
— George Swede

bordertown
breastfeeding mother
asks for a handout
— Alan Gettis

passport check:
my shadow waits
across the border
—George Swede

half-heard rain…
page after page
of family photos
—Gary Hothman

high autumn days
the morning glories open
to whatever comes
— Michael McClintock

home from the war
spaghetti and meatballs
piled high
— Michael McClintock

old bookstore
the key to the universe
only fifty cents
— Alexis Rotella

mountain appears
from behind the morning mist
just like that!
— Carl Genjo Bachmann

fading,
√ yearbook faces
I almost remember
— Adele Kenny

late autumn
√ choosing a suit
to be buried in
— Alan Gettis

steady rain
a turtle inside its shell
among the mossy stones
—George Swede

garden tilled:
we speak
of separating
—Alexis Rotella

a broken window
reflects half the moon,
half of me
— Michael McClintock

just the smell…
the flower stand,
empty now
— Michael McClintock

never leaving the mountainside
tiger lilies
blooming and dying
— Alan Gettis

sixty stories
of glass:
the summer moon
— Michael McClintock

unseen
the red sun sets
behind an old barn
— Carl Genjo Bachmann

in these deep woods,
no trace of me,
not even a footprint
— Adele Kenny

at the height of the argument
the old couple
pour each other tea
— George Swede

one mirror for everyone
the rest stop
restroom
—Gary Hothman

smell of incense
a hundred monks sit zazen
in well-worn robes
—Carl Genjo Bachmann

waking from
dreams of death:
egg scrambling sounds
— Alan Gettis

a wet spot
on the rock
where the frog sat
— Alexis Rotella

turtle pond:
what I thought were stones
begin to move
— Adele Kenny

used bookstore
a sunset beam lights a row
of forgotten authors
—George Swede

hidden by blankets
arguing with herself —
the bag lady
—Carl Genjo Bachmann

snowman's eye
sinking in
the spring rain
—Ruth Yarrow

coffee
in a paper cup—
a long way from home
—Gary Hotham

five or six freckles
on the sunny part
of her thigh
—Alan Gettis

two old men
help each other
up the steps
—Carl Genjo Bachmann

dandelion puff...
       still
        dandelion
— Adele Kenny

HAIKU BY CARL GENJO BACHMANN

"Iraqui Vet Please Help"
ignoring the homeless man
on my way to work

after an evening of scotch
dharma bums sit zazen
with big headaches

the windshield wipers' sound
comforts me driving home
from my brother's wake

back in town
the storekeeper
locks up for the night

walking in the woods
surprised by the full moon
we stop and stare

a late summer breeze
shatters the full moon
resting on the pond

HAIKU BY ALAN GETTIS

peddler's top hat—
the afternoon rain mixes
with nickels and dimes

autumn dusk..
even the magpies
are silent

spring breezes
old friends talk
of reincarnation

junkyard:
crows
in a '53 Chevy

at the pond
quoting Jesus and Buddha —
the honking geese

rain slowly
changing to snow…
a drifter asks directions

spring afternoon
on each end of the park bench
an old man sleeps

fish heads
the old butcher in his
bloodstained apron

meat market
seeing myself
in the window

street violinist
on his old top hat
the snow gathers

now and again
out of a hole in the ice
...seal heads

without you
separating the darks
from the whites

all-night diner
a Heinz bottle empties
into a Heinz bottle

leaving the zendo
feeling close to satori
a car cuts me off

asylum
Jesus preaching
to Jesus

backwoods cabin
a gutted dear hanging from
the barren elm

on the porch
the fat lady fans herself
with a fly swatter

fishing village wharf
through baskets of lobsters
the fog seeps...

spring dawn:
the living and the dead
arrive at the Ganges

listening to Mozart—
slicing zucchini
and my finger

abandoned farm
spring rain filling
the rusty wheelbarrow

the old man's black socks
all the way
to his Bermudas

flurries
a line forms outside
the soup kitchen

not listening to
the Zen lecture —
the Japanese maple

drought:
even the
milkcow

rainy morning
twenty years
between confessions

morning frost
the motel pumpkin
has no face

a single line
of sandpipers
become a haiku

snowed in:
adzuki beans soaking on
the potbelly stove

snowed in:
unfastening
her braid

just like that—
the great blue heron
at it again

ZEN

THE HISTORY OF ZEN

In his book *The Mindfulness Solution,* Ronald D. Siegel tells us how Buddhism was born.[1] Before he woke up and became Buddha, Siddhartha Guatama was the son of a king. When the prince was born, Brahmins examined him and concluded that Siddhartha was destined to become a great spiritual teacher. Because the king did not want this for his son, he sheltered, pampered, and protected him within the confines of the spacious palace grounds. He was only allowed to see and experience very pleasant things. The idea was that if Siddhartha did not experience pain, he would not be motivated to become a spiritual teacher.

However, one day Prince Siddhartha took an unsanctioned carriage ride outside the palace grounds—unsanctioned and uncensored. On this ride he was now unprotected from life's harsh realities. He saw a frail, toothless old person and asked his driver, "What's that?" The driver responded, "Old age." Siddhartha asked, "Who does that happen to?" The driver answered, "The lucky ones."

Next, the prince saw a sick man lying on the side of the road. He asked, "What's that?" The driver said, "Illness." Siddhartha queried, "And who does that happen to?" The driver said, "Mostly everyone in due time." Later that day, they saw vultures descending on a corpse. Prince Siddhartha asked, "What's that?" His driver answered, "Death." And when the prince then asked, "And who does that happen to?" the driver responded, "Everyone, I'm afraid."

That conversation and experience that took place in India during the fifth century led Siddhartha to begin years of intense meditation. He sought the path to overcome pain and suffering. According to legend, while sitting under the Bodhi tree in deep meditation, Buddha became enlightened when he experienced the oneness of the whole universe. After this experience, he did not become a recluse or ascetic; he became a spiritual teacher — awake, engaged, and compassionate.

Buddhism was based on this experience and Buddha's subsequent teachings. The core principle of these teachings was that to realize their essence required the practice of meditation. As Buddhism spread, meditation became its foundation. Over time, however, the practice of meditation began to lose its importance and was replaced with an emphasis on ritual, dogma, and social gathering.

In the sixth century, Zen (Ch'an in Chinese) arose as a movement to restore meditation as the foundation of Buddhist practice. For this reason, seated meditation became the heart of Zen practice. Zen flourished in China and in the seventh century spread south to Vietnam and northeast to Korea. By the twelfth century it had taken a foothold in Japan. At this time, Zen began to have a significant influence on Japanese culture. Spiritually and aesthetically, Zen permeated the tea ceremony, flower arrangement, calligraphy, haiku, wabi-sabi, and many other aspects of Japan's culture.

At the beginning of the twentieth century, Zen began to spread globally, particularly to Europe and the United States. Many Zen masters from the East came to the West to teach the way of Zen.

Zen is a special transmission outside the scriptures,
not founded upon words or letters.
By pointing directly to one's mind,
it lets one see into one's own true nature
and thus attain Buddhahood.
— Bodhidharma

Zazen (seated meditation) became the foundation of Buddhist teachings. To understand the influence of Zen, you must become familiar with its essence. This arises from the direct experience of reality through meditation rather than from Zen philosophy. What follows are key concepts to help you discover the essence of haiku and wabi-sabi and the heart of Zen.

INTIMATE ATTENTION

A student said to Master Ichu, "Please write for me something of great wisdom."

Master Ichu picked up his brush and wrote one word: *Attention*.

The student said, "Is that all?"

Master Ichu picked up his brush and wrote: *Attention, attention*.

The student became irritable. "That doesn't sound profound or subtle to me."

In response, Master Ichu wrote: *Attention, attention, attention*.

Frustrated, the student demanded, "What does the word attention mean?"

Master Ichu replied, "Attention means attention!"

The heart of Zen is paying attention. Paying attention to what? Paying attention to this moment right now. This moment is the only moment. The past is gone and the future has not yet arrived. There is only now! One of Japan's greatest Zen teachers and poets, Ryokan, said, "Look around! There is nothing besides this! Just this! Just this unfettered present moment."

Whatever the present moment offers is our life. To pay attention to the present is to live our lives fully. Master Dogen offers a way to pay attention when he says, "Imagine how present you would be if you were washing a baby." Imagine living your life this way. Of course, we don't always like what the present moment offers. For example, sickness, loss, unrest, violence, sadness, old age, death. Paying attention is the way to live with difficulties. If we fully pay attention, we can take the ingredients that are present in our lives and "make the best soup" possible from what life offers us.

In discussing the present moment, Jon Kabat Zinn points to great joy:

> It is a way of being, of seeing, of tapping into the full range of our humanity — often seen in playful children fully experiencing life in the here and now.[2]

> Zen Master Jizo asks Hogen, a wandering monk, "Where are you going?"
> Hogen answers, "I am on pilgrimage."
> Jizo asks, "What is the purpose of your pilgrimage?"
> Hogan replies, "I don't know."
> Jizo responds, "Not knowing is most intimate."
> — Case 20: *Book of Equanimity*[3]

A koan is an enigmatic, paradoxical story, statement, or question to be meditated on by the Zen student. It demonstrates the inadequacy of logical reasoning and is used to provoke enlightenment. What is the above koan pointing to?

Let's start with the mind that knows. It is a mind that is full of thoughts and ideas — and opinions. This mind is our daily companion. It creates the world we live in. The mind that creates thoughts, ideas, and opinions is the same mind that names and categorizes people and things. It identifies this as a floor, that as a window, and that as a door. It then categorizes these individual things as a building. It identifies one person as a man, another as a woman, and categorizes them as human beings. Certain people, based on their characteristics, are seen as friends, others as enemies. The mind that knows does this to everything that comes into awareness. This mind is very active and determines how we perceive the world. This perception is so commonsensical it is rarely challenged.

On a sunny afternoon in Manhattan, a man was on his lunch break when he encountered a middle-aged woman walking down the street in his direction. She was talking and singing to herself and was dressed in dirty, baggy clothes. Somewhat repulsed and uncomfortable, the man crossed the street to avoid her. What he was later to find out was that she was an actress rehearsing her part in an upcoming show. She was returning from a volunteer program that was creating a vegetable garden for a local homeless shelter.

The mind full of preconceptions colors our beliefs, perceptions, and experiences. On the other hand, the "not knowing mind" is a clear and unfettered mind. Not knowing is the path to intimacy because it is free of obstructions, like being able to see the valley after the fog has lifted. Without obstructions, we realize that nothing is separate from anything else—that everything is one. Being at one is the deepest form of intimacy—the deepest form of attention. It is an experience, not an idea.

Zen Master Dogen expressed the essence of this intimate attention when he said:

> We should handle each grain of rice
> as if we were handling our own eyes.

The ability to pay attention without obstructions requires cultivation. In this regard, Zen offers a practice to still the active mind. It's sitting meditation and is the practice of learning to pay attention. If it is practiced over time, the activity of the mind gradually quiets, and the door to intimacy opens.

The connection between the mind that knows and the mind

that doesn't know is explained by Korean Zen Master Seung Sahn:

> In a cookie factory, different cookies are baked in the shape of animals, cars, people, and airplanes. They all have different names and forms, but they are all made from the same dough, and they all taste the same.
>
> In the same way, all things in the universe — the sun, the moon, the stars, mountains, rivers, people, and so forth — have different names and forms, but they are all made from the same substance. The universe is organized into pairs of opposites: light and darkness, man and woman, sound and silence, good and bad. But all these opposites are mutual, because they are made from the same substance. Their names and their forms are different, but their substance is the same. Names and forms are made by your thinking. If you are not thinking and have no attachment to name and form, then all substance is one. Your don't-know mind cuts off all thinking. This is your substance.[4]

A haiku can be an expression of paying intimate attention to the present moment. It calls for a direct experience, which is very different than an intellectual understanding. When a haiku is written with a quiet mind, everyday activities are brought to life, and we have "just this."

> alone in the field
> a withered pine
> filled with sparrows
> — Carl Genjo Bachmann

Wabi-sabi is also an expression of paying intimate attention to the present moment. As emphasized earlier, wabi-sabi encourages the appreciation of things that are impermanent, imperfect, and incomplete. The beauty of these conditions can only be truly appreciated by paying intimate attention. For example, an old paint can lying on its side on the back porch. How many times have I (Bachmann) passed by this can and not noticed it? Intimate attention gives life to that old can — seeing the faded blue speckles, the beauty of the rusted rim, the dent on the side, and experiencing the bittersweet memory of painting my son's room. Paying attention in this intimate way allows us to fully experience and appreciate haiku, wabi-sabi, and life.

EQUANIMITY

Noah Levine says that we meet "the unpleasant, the neutral, and the pleasant with acceptance and understanding." This is how we can characterize equanimity. Equanimity is a state of stability or composure arising from a deep awareness and acceptance of the present moment. Zen teacher and Buddhist scholar Gil Fronsdal explains the origins of equanimity and how to cultivate it. The following is adapted from a talk he gave at the Insight Meditation Center, and is used here with his and their permission:

> Equanimity is one of the most sublime emotions of Buddhist practice. It is the ground for wisdom and freedom and the protector of compassion and love. While some may think of equanimity as dry neutrality or cool aloofness, mature equanimity produces a radiance and warmth of being. The Buddha described a mind filled with equanimity as abundant, exalted, immeasurable, without hostility and without ill-will.

> The English word *equanimity* translates two separate Pali words used by the Buddha. Each represents a different aspect of equanimity.

> The most common Pali word translated as equanimity is *upekkha*, meaning "to look over." It refers to the equanimity that arises from the power of observation—the ability to see without being caught by what we see. When well developed, such power gives rise to a great sense of peace.

> Upekkha can also refer to the ease that comes from seeing a bigger picture. Colloquially, in India the word was sometimes used to mean "to see with patience." We might understand this as "seeing with understanding." For example, when we know not to take offensive words person-

> ally, we are less likely to react to what was said. Instead, we remain at ease, or equanimous. This form of equanimity is sometimes compared to grandmotherly love. The grandmother clearly loves her grandchildren, but thanks to her experience with her own children, is less likely to be caught up in the drama of her grandchildren's lives.[5]

Dr. Fronsdal believes equanimity is remaining centered in the middle of the swirl of life, keeping our balance in the middle of whatever is happening. It's essentially keeping our balance in the middle of all that is. When we develop the capacity to respond with something resembling equanimity, we are less tossed around by our thoughts and emotions. Steeping ourselves in zazen helps us develop this capacity. We can still be passionate about our lives, loves, projects, and relationships, but we are no longer at the mercy of our thoughts or feelings.

Andrew Olendzki, a senior scholar at the Barre Center for Buddhist Studies, discusses how we cultivate equanimity when we mindfully focus on our breath. "It is engaging with the breath, or with a feeling tone, or with a thought, without simultaneously wanting it to stay as it is or wanting it to be different than it is." He goes on to say, "It may strike many of us as surprising, and even entirely alien, but the Buddhists are pointing to an intensity of emotional response that accepts and even celebrates what is happening, without trying to distort it into something else — into something that I prefer."[6]

There are many versions of the following story. It may have originally been told in the classic *Zen Flesh, Zen Bones*, by Paul Reps.

There was a monk named Hakuin who was well respected for his work among the people.

In the village, there lived a young woman, the daughter of the food sellers. The young woman became pregnant by her boyfriend, who worked nearby in the fish market. When the parents found out about this, they were very angry and pressured her to reveal the name of the father. She wanted to protect the young man and blurted the name of Hakuin as the father.

After the baby was born, the parents took the baby to Hakuin. They told Hakuin that he was responsible for the baby and left the infant with him. He responded, "Is that so?" And he simply accepted the responsibility for the child without further reaction.

The monk had no experience with babies, but he began to care for its needs, finding food, clothing, and warm shelter. The other villagers became angry with Hakuin for his offense, and his reputation was trashed. These comments did not affect Hakuin, who continued to put his effort and attention into the care of the baby.

After several years, the young woman was filled with remorse. She confessed to her parents the name of the true father. They immediately went to see Hakuin, apologized, and took the baby back with them. Hakuin watched as they returned to their home with the child he had cared for since birth and replied, "Is that so?"

Photo by Robert Morgans

When we look carefully, we can conclude that the world has always been a mess. There has always been trouble in paradise. As we previously discussed, the word *utopia* literally means "no place." In her book *Everyday Zen*, Charlotte Joko Beck writes about cultivating the ability to stand back from dualistic thinking, your feelings, and your problems, to become "a bigger container." By doing this, you are able to accommodate more of life. As you're able to accept more and more of life with less judgment, you're becoming a larger container that has room for your life and your feelings. You are able to hold more of life as it is.[7]

Pema Chodron reminds us that "...things don't really get solved. They come together and they fall apart. Then they come together again and fall apart again. It's just like that. The healing comes from letting there be room for all of this to happen: room for grief, for relief, for misery, for joy."[8]

Chodron suggests that the loose ends of our lives are never fully tied up:

> To be fully alive, fully human, and completely awake is to be continually thrown out of the nest. To live fully is to be always in no-man's-land, to experience each moment as completely new and fresh.[9]

Zenkei Blanch Hartman also talks about become a bigger container:

> If we're open to embracing the surprises as they arise, then there will be inconceivable joy. If we fuss and fume and say, "This isn't what I expected," then there will be inconceivable misery. Just to welcome your life as it arrives, moment after moment, to meet it as fully as you can, being as open to it as you can, being as ready for what arises as you can, meeting it wholeheartedly — this is renunciation. This is leaving behind all of your preferences, all your ideas and notions and schemes, just meeting life as it is.[10]

IMPERMANENCE

Photo by Robert Morgans

"Suzuki Roshi, I've been listening to your lectures for years," a student said during the question and answer time following a lecture, "but I just don't understand. Could you just please put it in a nutshell? Can you reduce Buddhism to one phrase?"

Everyone laughed. Suzuki laughed.

"Everything changes," he said. Then he asked for another question.[11]

Everything is in flux. The one thing we can count on is that everything changes. There is continual evolving and devolving, and all forms ruin sooner or later. As the adage reminds us, "This too shall pass." We are young, we bloom, we wither, and we die, as do our friends, families, children, and grandchildren. No one escapes. Death runs in my family and also in yours. We're all in the same boat. I (Gettis) experience this impermanence as a mandate to be kind, loving, and compassionate.

Facing decomposition, loss, and death are part of the bargain of being alive. If we want to experience the beauty, mystery, and awe of life, we need to also come to terms with inevitable losses. Wayne Muller addresses this:

> In that inevitable, excruciatingly human moment, we are offered a powerful choice. This choice is perhaps one of the most vitally important choices we will ever make, and it determines the course of our lives from that moment forward. The choice is this: will we interpret this loss as so unjust, unfair, and devastating that we feel punished, angry, forever and fatally wounded — or, as our heart, torn apart, bleeds its anguish of sheer, wordless grief, will we somehow feel this loss as an opportunity to become more tender, more open, more passionately alive, more grateful for what remains?[12]

In other words, can we be grateful for all of life and live our lives with a note of urgency? Can we let impermanence sink into our bones and marrow and our hearts and bellies? If we can't do this, we may live our lives the way Thich Nhat Hahn describes:

> In my mind I see a group of chickens in a cage, disputing over some seeds of grain, unaware that in a few hours they will be killed.[13]

Zazen can be the vehicle to take impermanence from a theoretical idea to an acute awareness that affects how we live our lives.

A zendo is a meditation hall where zazen is practiced. A gatha is a short verse or hymn that is chanted in the zendo to help us be mindful. The evening gatha says:

> Life and death are of supreme importance. Time passes swiftly by and opportunity is lost. Each of us must strive to awaken. Awaken. Take heed. Do not squander your life.

The root of "Buddha" is "budd," which means to wake up. So, Buddha was the one who woke up. It is not unusual for a Zen teacher to shout some variation of "Wake up!" We typically think that our lives will be sixty, seventy, or eighty years long. Optimists may think in terms of ninety or one hundred years. In reality, there is only this moment, right now! There are no guarantees beyond the present moment. Don't miss it! Korean Zen Master Seung Sahn would yell, "Soon dead!" in an effort to teach his students not to squander their lives.

An often-told Zen story has to do with the venerable, old teacher presiding over a funeral. After several minutes of silence, he shouts from his belly, "Who will be next?"

Life and impermanence are inseparable. They are joined at the hip. Paradoxically, impermanence assures that transformation occurs and that life continues, yet we are always at odds with this natural phenomenon. We want to hold on to everything and everyone we love. We want to hold on to our youth. We have a multi-billion-dollar anti-aging industry. Our unwillingness to accept aging and loss in its myriad of forms causes us to suffer and leads to anger, anxiety, pessimism, and unhappiness.

In her poem "The Summer Day," Mary Oliver asks:

> Doesn't everything die at last, and too soon?
> Tell me, what is it you plan to do
> with your one wild and precious life?[14]

The great Zen teacher Dogen captures the essence of impermanence:

> To what shall I
> liken the world?
> Moonlight reflected
> in dew drops,
> shaken from a crane's bill

A Zen student bought some beautiful flowers and placed them on the altar in a glass vase. Each morning she noticed subtle changes in the flowers. After a week, they had withered and died. She told her teacher of her sadness that something so beautiful could turn brown and die. The teacher remained silent for a bit before replying, "If you hold on to one moment and push away the next, you will not appreciate your life, and you will suffer."

Our mind is tempted to place more value on the newly bloomed flowers, and to see the past-their-prime flowers as old and unimportant. Each has its own beauty if we see them without preference. When we cling to the beautiful blooming flowers, we miss the teaching of impermanence offered by the dying ones. Impermanence is not a philosophical idea. It is a fact that applies to our life every day. We have no idea when we will find the road home closed. This incredible experience of being alive is fleeting. We should not push away any part of it. Accepting and embracing impermanence allows us to appreciate life from a wabi-sabi perspective.

In his book *Who Dies?*, Stephen Levine tells the following story, which I have taken the liberty of modifying slightly:

> Once someone asked a well-known Zen master, "In this world where everything changes, where nothing remains the same, where loss and grief are inherent in our very coming into existence, how can there be any happiness? How can we find security when we see that we can't count on anything being the way we want it to be?"
>
> The teacher, looking compassionately at this fellow, held up a gorgeous glass vase that had been given to him earlier in the morning and said, "You see this vase? For me, this vase is already broken. I enjoy it. It holds flowers admirably and sometimes reflects the sun in beautiful patterns.

If I should tap it, it has a lovely ring to it. But when I put this vase on a table and someone knocks into the table and the vase falls to the ground and shatters, I say, 'Of course.' When I understand that this beautiful new vase is already broken, every moment with it is precious. Every moment is just as it is, and nothing need be otherwise."[15]

ZAZEN

Why do we sit? The answer to this question varies. Some of us sit for peace of mind, some to have less anxiety or fear, or to reduce blood pressure or stress. Others sit to become enlightened or to understand the meaning of life. These are all compelling reasons. However, from a Zen point of view, these reasons are extra. In Zen we say the reason we sit is to "just sit." Anything else is extra and interferes with sitting. We don't sit to experience a particular outcome. We don't sit to attain or achieve something. We just sit! Just sitting is the heart of Zen practice.

If we create a goal for our sitting, what happens? We end up evaluating our progress. "This was a good sit. That was a bad sit. I'm not getting any better. Others are better at it than I am. I felt so peaceful yesterday. Today my mind won't be still!" This persistent evaluating interferes with "just sitting." It also subtly perpetuates a dualistic relationship with sitting. Sitting is something "I" do—which is different from just sitting. There is no "I" in just sitting. As Dogen taught, "To study the way is to study the self. To study the self is to forget the self."

So when we sit, we "just sit" with our whole body and mind, but holding no idea of sitting with our whole body and mind—no idea of attainment. We let go of our attachment to a causal relationship between sitting and enlightenment. We know enlightenment happens, but from the perspective of no causal relationship, enlightenment is an accident, and "just sitting" makes us accident-prone.[16] This advice is true for all activities. When we are eating, we just eat. When we are resting, we just rest. When we are walking, we just walk, and so forth.

Since we are so used to doing something to attain a result, this kind of advice sounds crazy and confusing. *Do something just to do it? No, I want peace of mind. I want less stress. I want to experience what the sages have experienced!* Because we tend to be so outcome oriented, this type of teaching can produce doubt, either in the practice or in one's self. The fact that this occurs is wonderful! If it happens to you, embrace it! Doubt is an entry point. It is when everything we know or think we know seems useless. Zen Master Hakuin, one of the most influential figures in Rinzai Zen, said, "At the bottom of great doubt lies great awakening. If you doubt fully, you will awaken fully."

When you realize you don't know, have faith in yourself and surrender to not knowing. You have reached the bare bones of practice. It's not necessary to tie yourself into knots trying to attain something. Simply make a whole-hearted and determined effort to "just sit."

> sitting quietly
> doing nothing
> spring comes
> and the grass grows by itself
> — Zenrin Kushu

Photo by Alan Gettis

after the storm
the Buddha in the garden
still sitting
— Alan Gettis

In his latest book, the Zen teacher and professor of Buddhism David R. Loy makes the following important point about meditation:

> One important human characteristic, apparently unique, is that we can develop the ability to dis-identify from anything and everything, letting go not only of the individual sense of separate self but also of collective selves as well: dissociating from patriarchy (I'm a man, not a woman), nationalism (I'm American, not Chinese), racism (I'm white, not black), even speciesism (I'm human, not a "lower animal"). Meditation encourages such nonattachment, of course, which is necessary to realize one's nondwelling mind. Yet the point of such letting go is not to dissociate from everything. It's just the opposite: by not taking this side rather than that, we become receptive to both. By not identifying with either, we can come to identify with everything.[17]

The noted Zen teacher Ezra Bayda writes passionately about active engagement with the present moment, whether we are focusing on our breath in meditation or immersed in the muddy water of life:

> It's pretty much a given that we will try to figure out what life is. We will say that life is difficult, or an opportunity. We might say that life is a gift, or a mystery. But all of these are just stories. We can posit meaning, and then try to live from that, but it's important to keep in mind that the meaning we posit is not an absolute—rather it is a practical response to the groundlessness of a world which seems to have no inherent meaning.

> This, as one author put it, is the existential dilemma—that we are beings who search for meaning and certainty in a universe that has neither.

> The question of meaning can certainly be a compelling motivator. When we feel a loss of direction or little sense of purpose, we may first use the usual props—such as busyness, entertainments and distractions—to cover over the feeling of emptiness inside. When these props don't work, we may go to therapy or come to spiritual practice, to address the experience of an inner aimlessness in our lives.

> When we feel helpless and anxious about the inner chaos in our lives we naturally want to find answers to feel some sense of comfort and control. But we don't just want an intellectual answer to the meaning of life; we also want to know what to do—how to actually live.

> Here's what it comes down to: we are wired to live, not

just to think, and we need to engage in meaningful activity for the question of meaning to no longer matter.

From the point of view of Zen practice, the question: "What is the meaning of life?" is like a koan, where the practice is to sit and be present with the question itself. Not to focus on getting an answer, but to just stay with the question. To stay with the question, with the visceral experience of the anxiety and confusion of not knowing, is where the question can eventually resolve itself. It resolves itself through the doing—from sitting with the physicality of our present moment experience.

As we truly reside in this physical experience, at some point it may be like popping a balloon, where the anxiety and confusion and need to know just disappear. When this happens, the feeling that life will never be enough is no longer an issue.

This is what sitting in meditation has always been about— staying with our present moment experience. We don't have to have an explanation for why sitting is good for us. We can say that sitting still in meditation helps settle the body and mind, but the fact is, until we sit and experience this for ourselves, no explanation will satisfy us. The satisfaction comes from the doing. The meaning comes from the activity. We can add on explanations after—that may help somewhat with our answer-seeking mind. But again, the real answer comes from how we live. In a way, all genuine spiritual practices answer the question of how to live.[18]

How does meditation practice affect a person's daily life? In the early 1970s I (Gettis) would regularly meditate at a small New York City zendo at the edge of Greenwich Village. We sat on our cushions for the designated length of time, and when we finished, we would put our cushions in wall racks constructed specifically to hold those cushions. So we got off our cushions and went back out into the marketplace to deal with the real world, so to speak. We waited in lines, took public transportation, dealt with a variety of people, did our jobs, went home to our families, and so on.

What a relief to get back to the zendo, where we could find time to destress and sit quietly. That's how it begins. A funny thing happens after years of being steeped in meditation. You meditate, put your cushion in the rack, and go into the marketplace, but now, it's as if that cushion is stuck to your behind. Yes, it's a startling discovery when you realize that your practice is your life.

The story of Big Fred is a wonderful example of bringing practice into your life.

> I used to have an upstairs neighbor, an old, overweight ex-boxer with bad knees, who worked as a janitor. Fred would generally come home with his groceries, a couple of six-packs, and a stack of lottery tickets while I was in the middle of my evening meditation; through my door I would hear his labored breathing and the clanking of his beer bottles as he struggled up the stairs. At first I tried to ignore it. Then, as the contradiction grew more embarrassing, came annoyance — I would jump up and help him, but resent the fact that my practice had once again been interrupted. Because I'm a slow learner, it took a few weeks before I realized, This *is* the practice. If I have to sit cross-legged on a cushion to experience boundlessness, that's a boundary. Hauling beer up the stairs is the meditation, and Big Fred is the teacher.[19]

Robert Aitken Roshi perhaps said it best. He said that he was not so interested in the day you attained enlightenment as much as he was interested in the day after!

The noted Zen teacher James Ishmael Ford pares meditation down to its barest essentials. He parsimoniously and simply tells you, "Sit down. Shut up. Pay attention."[20] Of course, it's not as easy as it sounds, but that is all it takes to begin. Ishmael advises us to sit straight up, whether we sit on a cushion on the floor or on a chair. He says, "It helps to have your bottom a little higher than your knees." Put your hands on your lap, and with your eyes partially open, gaze at the floor about four feet in front of you. You have just finished Step One: Sit down.

We incessantly talk silently to ourselves. We call this thinking. That brings us to Step Two: Shut up. As you concentrate on following your inhalations and exhalations, you may notice thoughts. Just witness them without judgment, and return all your awareness to your breath. Every thought is treated exactly the same; the content of the thought is irrelevant.

Step Three: Pay attention. Simply focus on your breathing, paying full attention to the inhalation and the exhalation. When thoughts arise, gently let them go and return your focus to your breath. Shunryu Suzuki Roshi says it best:

Leave your front door and your back door open.
Allow your thoughts to come and go.
Just don't serve them tea.

ACCEPTANCE

There is a Taoist story of a farmer whose horse ran away. That evening, his neighbors gathered at his farmhouse to offer their condolences on his bad luck. He said, "May be." The following day, the horse returned and brought with it six wild horses. All the neighbors came by to congratulate the farmer on his good fortune. He said, "May be."

The next morning his sixteen-year-old son tried to ride one of the wild horses. He was thrown and broke his leg. Again the neighbors came to offer their sympathy for his misfortune. The farmer said, "May be." The following afternoon, army officers came to the village to seize young men to fight in an unjust war. The farmer's son was rejected because of his broken leg. When the neighbors came in to say how fortunate everything had turned out, the farmer said, "May be."

We can live life passionately and deeply without overreacting to every new development that seems to offer obstacles to hurdle. Keep this story in mind. When something happens and your first inclination is to say, "Why me?" see if instead you can possibly say, "May be."

It is not the circumstances we find ourselves in that cause suffering, but rather what we tell ourselves about those circumstances.

This is it. No matter how much
the mind wishes it were otherwise.
— Carl Genjo Bachmann

One of the most difficult things in life is to accept it as it is. We spend most of our lives wishing things could be different than they are. It is the equivalent of wrestling with Jesus, Buddha, God, and the Universe. It's been said that serenity or something resembling peace of mind comes from trading your expectations and preferences for acceptance.

Of course, we are not advocating a nonchalant or passive attitude toward life. We still need to find purpose and meaning and live our lives in an engaged and passionate manner. We can still rail against injustice, protest, and the like while we paradoxically and simultaneously cultivate acceptance. If this seems like a koan to you, I understand.

In his book *Solid Ground: Buddhist Wisdom for Difficult Times*, Zen teacher Norman Fischer writes:

> Accepting suffering as part of our lives doesn't mean we give up hope or stop wanting some things to be different. For example, if someone you love is diagnosed with cancer, of course you will hope and search for a cure. You can accept the fact of the diagnosis at the same time that you do everything possible to ameliorate it. There is no contradiction between acceptance and hope. In fact, acceptance and hope are connected. Acceptance is not resignation. Acceptance is a lively engagement with conditions as they are.[21]

Cultivating acceptance means we gradually learn to let go. We let go of our need to control. We let go of our wish that life be different than it is. When we cling to the idea that life should be more the way we want it to be, we are evidencing thoughts and feelings of entitlement. George Orwell said, "Happiness can exist only in acceptance." That must include self-acceptance, to compassionately open up to yourself in all your splendor and uniqueness, including your flaws, foibles, and idiosyncrasies. Even if you want to work on modifying certain aspects of yourself, acceptance is a prerequisite for change.

In Zen it is recited:

> May we exist like a lotus,
> at home in the muddy water.
> Thus we bow to life as it is.

It is when we bow to "life as we think it should be" or "life as we'd like it to be" that we suffer.

A well-known Zen story tells of two monks walking in a heavy rain on a dirt road. They came upon a young woman in a silk kimono who was unable to cross a very muddy section. The one monk swiftly lifted her and carried her over the mud. The two monks continued on their way, walking in silence until hours later when they approached the monastery grounds.

The second monk could no longer restrain himself and said, "What's wrong with you? We monks don't go near women, especially not young and lovely ones. Why did you do that?"

To which the first monk replied, "I put her down hours ago. Are you still carrying her?"

Jack Kornfield tells the story of his asking a Zen master if he ever gets angry. The master replied, "Of course I get angry, but then a few minutes later I say to myself, 'What's the use of this?' and I let it go."

> Let it go or be dragged.
> — Zen proverb

When we let go of the past and our regrets, resentments, guilt, and shame, and when we let go of our expectations that life should treat us better, and when we let go of our need to control, and when we let go of our fears of the future, and when we let go of blaming, judging, and comparing, we give ourselves permission to be happier. Happiness is less related to what we acquire and more related to what we let go of. By choosing to let go, we choose freedom to move on. Control is an illusion. We don't know what will happen five minutes from now. Whatever happens, we need to trust we'll be able to figure it out and deal with it to the best of our abilities. That's the closest we can get to any feeling of security in our impermanent and imperfect existence.

It is important to let go because it frees us up to have more energy and to experience more joy. As it turns out, the pain is in the holding on, not the letting go. A Zen proverb has it that wisdom is letting go of something every day.

I (Gettis) love the following story, written by Guri Mehta and used here with her permission. It is about a lesson in letting go that she learned from her mother. I think Guri's mother was a wonderful teacher:

> As a teen, there were many days where I hovered across the kitchen counter, watching my mom make fresh *roti* (Indian bread), ready to grab one as soon as it fluffed on the open flame. Of course, she would snatch it right back to spread a little butter on top before giving it back. Like a half-starved child, I would plunge right into the soft bread like no one had fed me for days. There's nothing like your mom's cooking. And my favorite was the round hot *rotis* with *sabji* (curried veggies), and thick *Punjabi dal* (lentils).

> Within minutes of me stepping in the door, there would be the inevitable question of *"roti banawa?"* Should I make *roti?* The *sabji* and the *dal* were ever-ready in our house, but the *rotis* were usually made fresh each meal. Like all Indian moms of that generation, she had her process. She would carefully break a small part of the kneaded dough, roll it into a small round ball between her palms, spread it into a disk-shape with her hands. Then using a wooden rolling pin, methodically roll it into a perfect circle on a *chakla* (usually wooden but in her case, a round carved white marble). She would then carefully place it

onto the round griddle on the stove, followed by the open flame to fluff it. With the next one already rolled out, this was the time for catching up about the day. The one thing that was unique about her process was that she never rushed — she made them slowly, gently caring for each one as if everything in life rested on that one *roti*. Mom would sometimes even rest her left hand on her hip like she had all the time in the world, and hold a rolled roti in the other — and chat with me while at the same time keeping an eye on the *roti* on the stove.

About seven-eight years ago, we were hosting a get-together at my parents' home, and like most *Punjabis* (actually I think all), she has a second stove set up in the garage. I wish I'd kept to myself that day, but I was trying to be of some help to her. We were running a bit behind schedule, and she was just about finished with everything else, so now we just needed to make the *rotis* before the guests started arriving. I tried to work quickly, knowing that I was probably rushing her. As I was hurriedly moving everything closer to the table next to the stove, something happened that I wish I had the power to undo. The marble *chakla* that I've always seen her use slipped out of my hand and fell hard on the concrete garage floor. It made a loud sound as soon as it hit the surface, and broke into several pieces.

It was obvious right away that there was no way of salvaging it. I was shocked at my absent-mindedness and felt horrible as my mom looked over her shoulder to see what had happened. All I could muster was, "Oh, Mom, I'm so sorry. I don't know what happened." She was quiet for a second and then just said, *"Koi ghal nahi,"* her version of "It's okay." She then walked over quietly, picked up the broken pieces, and put them in the trash can in the garage. Quickly grabbing a smooth cutting board, she started rolling the *rotis*. We continued with the rest of the evening, and she didn't say anything else about the matter.

A few days later, as we sat down for tea, I still felt bad and wondered if I could find a replacement. I brought it up again, but she said don't worry about it, what's done is done. When asked how long she had it, she casually mentioned that she had it for a while. Her grandmother had taught her how to make *rotis* on it. I felt so bad, and I'll never forget the look in her eyes when she gently confided, "It belonged to my mother." Her mother! Who she rarely talks about because she doesn't have any memories of her. Her mother who had passed away when Mom was an infant, and she was raised by her grandmother and step-mom.

My older sister later told me that the marble *chakla* was given to her mother by her parents when she got married, and it was the last thing that my mom had left that belonged to her mom (and her entire lineage). She brought it with her from India to the US when our family migrated here.

As my mom and I sipped tea that day, she shared none of this. Focused on making me feel better, with the wave of her hand, she just said, *"Jaan de"* (let it go), as she poured me more tea and asked about my day. Even now when I think about this, tears well up. If I was in her place, there's no way I would've not said anything. There would have at least been a lecture or two about being more mindful, there would've been anger, or guilt for a little while about something so precious now gone forever.

As I recall this now, I feel like her reaction to this so aptly sums up who she is. Someone who goes through the ups and downs in life with resilience, selflessness, always focusing on what's good, and what's happening right instead of what went wrong. Someone who clearly knows that what is done cannot be undone, but instead of looking at the broken pieces of the past, you put them in their place, and just keep on moving forward with all the grace that you can muster.[22]

SACRED GROUND

There is a Zen proverb, "After enlightenment, the laundry." Does this suggest that we go from the divine to the mundane? Well, unless you decide to spend the rest of your life as a recluse sitting on a mountaintop in the Himalayas, the "laundry" and all that it connotes awaits you. The laundry in this case represents all the chores, obligations, and responsibilities that we typically pay limited, non-focused attention to, because we don't deem them to be spiritual or important. Paying bills, making lunches, getting gas, weeding the garden, waiting in line at the supermarket, and so on. These ordinary experiences are thought to be boring, unimportant, and unrelated to spirituality and our sense of well-being. Unfortunately, these "unimportant" events that we think have little value take up seventy to eighty percent of our lives. Stop. Think about that. You are living the overwhelming majority of life as if it doesn't matter that much. You only seem to value the small percentage that contains the vacation in Europe, taking the kids to Disney World, getting a pedicure, seeing the Broadway show, eating the gourmet meal, celebrating holidays, and the like.

What if we approached life as if there were no intermission, as if there were no unimportant moments? What if we realized that wherever we are and whomever we're with, it is fertile ground for awakening? What if we realized that we are always on sacred ground and that all we ever do is go from one (w)holy place to another? What if we paid attention without judgment and without preconceived notions to waiting in line at the supermarket, and truly stayed connected to and engaged with that experience? Dogen wrote, "Each activity is sacred." It is holy or whole just as it is.

When we stop judging and evaluating ourselves and others with our critical self-conscious minds, we may get in touch with our non-dualistic, nonjudgmental mind. The self drops away, producing a selfless communion with whatever circumstances we find ourselves in and whomever we are with. Egocentricity dissolves and awe may emerge, but we still need to do the laundry.

The Zen teacher Albert Low offers additional perspective on why each act is sacred:

> When we see life itself as meaningful, we will prize the process of attaining a result as much as the result itself. Preparing the water, washing the dishes, drying them and setting them in order in the cupboard will all be meaningful actions and performed for their own sake. Each moment of the day would have its own worth.[23]

NOTHING SPECIAL

The enigmatic Zen master Rinzai spoke of the true man of no rank, and the story became a koan that Zen disciples have pondered for centuries. When our minds make better or worse, this or that, and we engage in labeling everything we encounter, we think we know the truth—we think we have a high rank. Our dualistic thinking reinforces that we are special either because of our intellects, talents, appearance, wealth, or status, or that we are special due to being victims.

The noted teacher Sandy Boucher writes, "In the dining room of the meditation hall where I first encountered Buddhist practice, a stuffed green and scarlet parrot hung from the ceiling. It gripped a sign in its beak that read, 'We are in training to be nobody special.'"[24] Aren't we really in training to become someone special? As it turns out, reading the Bible, traveling to India, and doing countless hours of meditation don't make us special. John Cage's favorite Zen story is about the Zen master who said, "Now that I'm enlightened, I'm just as miserable as I ever was!"

When we are constantly labeling in a dichotomous manner, we are sitting in judgment of ourselves and others. When we are busy judging, there is little room for compassion and perception free of distortion. We are very busy building up and protecting our egos. It's been said, "No ego. No problems." The more realistic position might just be to be aware of your ego and to check it at the door.

When Shunryu Roshi was asked, "How much ego do you need?" he replied, "Just enough so that you don't step in front of a bus."

One day a rabbi, in a frenzy of religious passion, rushed in before the ark, fell to his knees, and started beating his breast, crying, "I'm nobody! I'm nobody!"

The cantor of the synagogue, impressed by this example of spiritual humility, joined the rabbi on his knees, saying, "I'm nobody! I'm nobody!"

The custodian, watching from the corner, couldn't restrain himself either. He joined the other two on his knees, calling out, "I'm nobody! I'm nobody!"

At which point the rabbi, nudging the cantor with his elbow, pointed at the custodian and said, "Look who thinks he's nobody!"[25]

If we are able to catch a glimpse of the world undivided into names and categories (as sometimes happens), we might at least temporarily become a person of no rank who is nobody special. The ten thousand become one. David Chadwick, in *Zen Is Right Here*, cites the following story:

One day while editing a transcription of Suzuki Roshi's first lecture on the *Sandokai*, I came upon the phrase "things as it is." I asked him if perhaps he had meant to say "things as they are," which I thought to be proper syntax.

"No, he said, "what I meant is 'things as it is.'"

COMPASSIONATE ENGAGEMENT

Hozan Alan Senauke, a Zen priest and poet, writes:

> Life has no particular meaning. Or it is far beyond my abil-
> ity to see the entirety of it. The question is: what will I do
> with the life that has been given to me? Will I serve life,
> and all that is in it? Or will I wait to be served? Moment by
> moment, breath by breath, I face this choice.[26]

What we choose and what we pay attention to determines the
quality as well as the meaning of our lives. Even though we make
what seem to be "good" choices, and even when we pay attention
to the "right" things, our lives may still be messy and complicated.
Spiritual life has to do with our willingness to open ourselves to
whatever is presented to us — the whole, holy mess. Most spiritual
practices are about compassion and engagement with life as it is.

There is a story of four men, who after a long journey, come
to a high wall surrounding a village. Not knowing what was on
the other side, they climb to the top to see what is there. First one,
then another, and then the third are delighted by what they see.
It is a veritable paradise. They each scale the wall and jump into
the compound. Not so with the fourth. Equally delighted by what
he saw, this one remembers those he had left behind and returns
to tell them what he had seen and how to get there. This person is
a bodhisattva — the person who could attain nirvana but chooses
instead to stay in this world to help enlighten others because of
the compassion that he feels toward them.

Legend has it that bodhisattvas can assume an infinite number of roles and disguises in order to help set you free from psychological and spiritual obstacles that hold you back and interfere with your waking up. They continually present you with opportunities to work on yourself. For example, if your anger causes problems for you, bodhisattvas may arise now and then so as to provide you with chances to learn to see things differently. In this light, the driver who cuts you off, the telemarketer who calls during dinner, or the rude woman at the supermarket may all be regarded as bodhisattvas. Instead of becoming enraged, you can realize that these people are actually helping you to think less dualistically and feel less angry. Now, you can smile, feel compassion, and say to yourself, "Thank you, bodhisattva, for this valuable opportunity."

GRATITUDE

There is a room in the basement of my house that I (Bachmann) use as a mini-zendo. It has bookcases filled with books, photographs, artifacts, and statues that I have acquired over the years. In keeping with the simplicity of Zen, I have just a few prints hanging on the walls. My favorite is a framed print of the Chinese *Cold Mountain* poets, Han Shan and Shih Te. Each morning after breakfast I go down to my little zendo to sit. It is an act of love.

Last week, as I walked down the basement stairs, in front of me was a small swatch of sunlight on the wall. It was the shape of the small basement window through which the sunlight came. In this moment it was all there was. My mind stopped thinking, and there was "just this," without any thought of "just this." Suddenly I was filled with gratitude, just for being alive. The experience was not dramatic; it was very simple.

We all are part of this splendid interdependent web in which we exist. We belong and are part of everything, and everything is a part of us. Out of the realization of this, true love and compassion grow, which can be a deep source of gratitude.

Gratitude doesn't always come from profound insights. Many times life presents itself in a very simple and ordinary way. We may be sitting across the table from our son or daughter as they eat their morning bowl of oatmeal. Then, all of a sudden, we are overcome by love and gratitude for their being there.

In the zendo we ring the gong and are filled with the sound. "Bong!" We are filled with the gratitude for being in this precious moment. There is a Buddhist prayer that goes: "May I be given the appropriate difficulties so my heart can truly open with compassion." No less than, the Dalai Lama said, "Remember that not getting what you want is sometimes a wonderful stroke of luck."

Can we feel gratitude for all our failures, understanding that they are our teachers? We say in Zen, "Mind makes." What we tell ourselves about the pain we're in can determine whether or not it is the enemy or a teacher. If we tell ourselves it is a teacher, we will suffer less and perhaps experience gratitude for its arrival. Being able to feel grateful in times of difficulty prevents us from being victims.

Gratitude is a gift. We should let it inspire us to act on it. We should let it inspire us in our daily lives to reach out to others with an open heart. I feel deeply grateful to be alive. My challenge is, when I see someone suffering, can I use this life for which I feel so grateful to reach out to them?

Living a life of gratitude changes your life. Omraam Mikhaël Aïvanhov says, "The day I acquired the habit of consciously pronouncing the words 'thank you,' I felt I had gained the possession of a magic wand capable of transforming everything." It is a wonderful feeling when you awaken to Suzuki Roshi's realization that just being alive is enough. Zenkei Blanche Hartman writes beautifully about this experience in her book *Seeds for a Boundless Life: Zen Teachings from the Heart*. After a heart attack and a hospital stay, she stepped into the sunshine and had a sudden realization that she could be dead and that "the rest of my life is just a gift."

Aren't we all on borrowed time? Aren't all of our days numbered? When we let this sink into our bones and marrow and realize there is so much to be grateful for, it becomes our default setting.

> For example: I (Gettis) woke up this morning (thank you for another day). I woke up without a headache or a toothache. No stiff neck either (I'm thankful). There was fresh fruit and cereal in the house. The coffee pot worked. The treadmill worked. The shower worked. We weren't out of shampoo or toothpaste or soap.

> It's easy to pay attention and become emotionally charged when these things are not there. But, how about the flip side—noticing and feeling good and expressing gratitude when the normal day-to-day things occur: The car started right away. I didn't get a flat on the way to the office, and I didn't lock my keys in the car when I got out (I feel appreciative). I began seeing patients (feeling grateful I'm healthy enough to work all day). The phones were working. The computer was not down. The fax machine was operating. "Rubbernecking" to see all the things I take for granted and to express my thanks.[27]

If you are reading this you are alive. You have been given another day. Many haven't. If you have a pulse, you have something to be grateful for. Regardless of whether we are theists or atheists, and regardless of our unique set of problems and circumstances, we are alive and there is hope. When we are grateful, what we have is enough.

> In life as in dance, grace glides on blistered feet.
> —Alice Abrams

Ruben L. F. Habito, a Zen master and professor of world religions and spirituality at Perkins School of Theology equates boundless gratitude with the meaning of life:

> There is no "meaning of life" apart from living it, breath by miraculous breath, moment by wondrous moment. It's welcoming every day as a new day, opening one's heart to the infinite dwelling in each here and now. It's the quiet joy of just being, earnestly wishing, may all be well, may all beings be well.
>
> Hearing the cries of the world, it's crying out from one's own pain with all those in pain. It's offering a helping hand, not letting the other hand know. It's seeing a child smile, and smiling back. It's being hurt, and refraining from hurting back. It's being loved, and loving back with all one's got. It's growing up, getting old, getting sick, dying, bowing out, with palms joined, heart filled with boundless gratitude. And through all this, knowing, deep within, all shall be well, all manner of thing shall be well.[28]

EPILOGUE

Empty-handed I entered the world.
Barefoot I leave it.
My coming, my going—
Two simple happenings that got entangled.
—Kozan Ichikyo, 1360

Out beyond ideas of wrongdoing
and rightdoing there is a field.
I'll meet you there.
—Rumi

The haiku mind, the wabi-sabi mind, and the Zen mind all accept what is before us, without sentimentality and without adding anything extra.

> the legs of the crane
> have become short
> in the summer rains
> — Basho

> on a pine branch
> a disheveled hawk
> waits out the rainstorm
> — Carl Genjo Bachmann

Wabi-sabi, haiku, and Zen teach us "Just this." We come to appreciate what is, and intimately know that what is before us is the truth of that moment. When we stop lamenting the transient and give up our attachments to how we think life should be, we can begin to fully accept, appreciate, and embrace life, just as it is. Eiko Joshin Carolyn Atkinson expresses this poignantly in her poem "This Is What There Is":

> This is what there is:
> Waking in the dark and cold. No more sleep.
> This is what there is:
> Rain on the roof. Newspaper soaked and muddy.
> His mouth trembles as he thinks of children suffering.
> Autumn leaves, red-yellow, suddenly changing.

> This is all there is:
> Sitting down again and again, in the dark, in the cold,
> In the sun, in the rain — this is all there is.
> Hair turning silver, teachers dying, lovers leaving, old

friends returning.
Grown children calling to say, "I love you."

This is what we have:
Cold ocean breeze, salt in the air.
A mother cries out, calling her son a fool.
This is what we have:
A friend eating soup across the table.
A struggle to praise this mutilated world.
A wish for transcendent meaning. A desire to change our
lives.
And this desire—is what we have too:
A wish for the heart to heal, the mind to relax—
This, too, is our life.

It can't be right, can it?
But, this is all there is:
Unopened mail, unfinished lives.
Grief, pain, unexpected joy.
Green tea. Shivering. Fog rising from the land.
Wishing to be elsewhere.
The moon at the window.

This is *all* there is: birth, death, and everything that lies
between.
Nothing special. Everything special. Nothing other than
just . . . what . . . it is.
This is all there is.

This is what we have: life, as it is.
Late-season roses, jasmine.
Learning to love these ordinary lives.
Shoes. We have shoes.

This is what we have. This is what there is. This is it. This is it.[29]

What is the teaching "Just this"? *Just this* means nothing extra. "Just this!" It is paying full attention without identifying the experience. "This" is nameless. When we eat we just eat. When we sweep we just sweep. When we walk we just walk. We experience each moment wholeheartedly, just as it is.

daffodils
so beautiful
left unnamed

Only just this.

WABI-SABI NOTATIONS

1. Red Pine. *The Mountain Poems of Stonehouse.* Copper Canyon Press, 2014, p. 161.

2. Ando, T. "What Is Wabi-Sabi?" nobleharbor.com/tea/chado/WhatIsWabi-Sabi.htm.

3. Gold, T. *Living Wabi-Sabi.* Andrews McMeel Publishing, 2004, p. xii.

4. Koren, L. *Wabi-Sabi for Artists, Designers, Poets & Philosophers.* Stone Bridge Press, 1994, p. 62.

5. Koren, L. "A Culture of Simplicity." Resurgence & Ecologist, Issue 203, Nov/Dec, 2000, p. 7.

6. Powell, R. stillinthestream.com.

7. Ando, T. "What Is Wabi-Sabi?" nobleharbor.com/tea/chado/WhatIsWabi-Sabi.htm.

8. Ando, T. "What Is Wabi-Sabi?" nobleharbor.com/tea/chado/WhatIsWabi-Sabi.htm.

9. Koren, L. *Wabi-Sabi for Artists, Designers, Poets & Philosophers.* Stone Bridge Press, 1994, pp. 46, 49.

10. Koren, L. *Wabi-Sabi for Artists, Designers, Poets & Philosophers.* Stone Bridge Press, 1994, p. 21

11. Gold, T. *Living Wabi-Sabi.* Andrews McMeel Publishing, 2004, p. 16.

HAIKU NOTATIONS

1. Akmakjian, H. *Snow Falling from a Bamboo Leaf: The Art of Haiku.* Capra Press, 1979, p. 11.

2. Akmakjian, H. *Snow Falling from a Bamboo Leaf: The Art of Haiku.* Capra Press, 1979, p. 35.

3. Sahn, S. *Dropping Ashes on the Buddha* (compiled and edited by Stephen Mitchell). Grove Press, 1976, p. xi.

4. Henderson, S. "How Many?" poemhunter.com.

5. Aitken, R. *A Zen Wave: Basho's Haiku and Zen.* Shoemaker & Hoard, 2003.

6. Rossetti, C. G. "On the Death of a Cat." poemhunter.com

7. McClintock, M. Used with his permission.

8. Watts, A. *The Way of Zen.* Vintage Books, 1957, p. 231.

9. Adam, M. *Wandering in Eden.* Alfred A. Knopf, 1976, p. 81.

10. Heuvel, Cor van den. *The Haiku Anthology.* Simon & Schuster, 1986, p. 74.

11. Red Pine. *The Mountain Poems of Stonehouse*. Copper Canyon Press, 2014.

ZEN NOTATIONS

1. Siegel, R. *The Mindfulness Solution: Everyday Practices for Everyday Problems.* The Guilford Press, 2009, pp. 16 – 17.

2. Kabat-Zinn, J. *Wherever You Go, There You Are: Mindfulness Meditation in Everyday Life.* Hyperion, 1994.

3. Wick, G. S. *The Book of Equanimity: Illuminating Classic Zen Koans.* Wisdom Publications, 2005, Case 20.

4. Sahn, S. *Dropping Ashes on the Buddha* (compiled and edited by Stephen Mitchell). Grove Press, 1976.

5. Fronsdale, G. insightmeditationcenter.org. Adapted from a talk, May 29, 2004. Used with permission from Insight Meditation Center.

6. Olendzki, A. "The Buddha's Smile: Cultivating Equanimity." Tricycle, Winter 2012.

7. Beck, C. J. *Everyday Zen.* Harper Collins, 2007.

8. Chödrön, P. *The Pocket Pema Chödrön.* Shambhala, 2008, p. 88.

9. Chödrön, P. *When Things Fall Apart: Heart Advice for Difficult Times.* Shambhala, 2008.

10. Hartman, Z. B. *Seeds for a Boundless Life: Zen Teachings from the Heart*. Shambhala, 2015.

11. Chadwick, D. *Zen Is Right Here: Teaching Stories and Anecdotes of Shunryu Suzuki*. Shambhala, 2017.

12. Muller, W. *A Life of Being, Having, and Doing Enough*. Three Rivers Press, 2010.

13. McLeod, M. *The Best Buddhist Writing 2009*. "The World We Have" by Thich Nhat Hanh, p. 70.

14. Oliver, M. *New and Selected Poems*. Beacon Press, 1992.

15. Levine, S and O. *Who Dies? An Investigation of Conscious Living and Conscious Dying*. Anchor, 1989.

16. Widely attributed to Suzuki Roshi.

17. Loy, D. "The Meaning of It All." excellencereporter.com, 2015.

18. Bayda, E. *Beyond Happiness: The Zen Way to True Contentment*. Shambhala, 2010.

19. Sluyter, Dean. *The Zen Commandments: Ten Suggestions for a Life of Inner Freedom*. Penguin Putnam, 2001.

20. Ford, J. I. "I Want to Be Peaceful." Shambhala Sun, July 2012, pp. 33 – 35.

21. Boorstein, S., Fischer, N., and Rinpoche, T. *Solid Ground: Buddhist Wisdom for Difficult Times*. Parallax Press, 2011.

22. gurimehta.blogspot.com, November 19, 2017.

23. Low, A. "Life Has No Meaning—But Life Is Intensely Meaningful." excellencereporter.com, July 2015.

24. Boucher, S. "We Are in Training to Be Nobody Special." Tricyle/Trike Daily, December 2017.

25. Kurtz, E. and Ketcham, K. The Spirituality of Imperfection: *Storytelling and the Search for Meaning.* Bantam, 2002.

26. Senauke, H. A. "What Is the Meaning of Life?" excellencereporter.com, July 2015.

27. Gettis, A. *The Happiness Solution: Finding Joy and Meaning in an Upside Down World.* Goodman Beck Publishing, 2008.

28. Atkinson, E. J. C. "This Is What There Is." excellencereporter.com, May 2016.

PERMISSIONS

Thank you to all the haiku poets who agreed to let us use their work: Gary Hothman, George Swede, Alexis Rotella, Ruth Yarrow, Michael McClintock.

Adele Kenny's haiku from her book *Not Asking What If*, Muse-Pie Press, 2016. Used with her permission.

Haiku from the Japanese Masters appeared in *Sun-Faced Haiku Moon-Faced Haiku* by Alan Gettis and were based on R. H. Blyth's translations published by Hokuseido Press.

Thank you to Leonard Koren, the ultimate authority on wabi-sabi, for his generous permission to use material from his book *Wabi-Sabi for Artists, Designers, Poets & Philosophers*.

Thank you to Nicolae Tanase, the founder of Excellence Reporter (excellencereporter.com), for his permission to use the material from his website, which appears in his book *What Is the Meaning of Life?: A Journey into the Wisdom of Life*, 2017.

Thank you to Eiko Joshin Carolyn Atkinson for her beautiful and poetic writings used in our epilogue.

ABOUT THE AUTHORS

Alan Gettis has been a practicing psychologist for 50 years and is still learning. He is a past vice-president of the Haiku Society of America, and his haiku have been published in journals throughout the world, including the United States, Australia, Canada, and Japan. This is his sixth book.

Sensei Carl Genjo Bachmann is a zen teacher in the white plum lineage. He received dharma transmission from Robert Kennedy Roshi. He is the teacher and one of the founders of the Clear Mountain Zen Center (ClearMountainZen.org) in Montclair, New Jersey. Carl also maintains his practice as a psychotherapist.

ABOUT THE ARTIST

Cyndi Goetcheus Sarfan, a.k.a. CJ Newlife, is a fine art and nature photographer currently living on the Outer Banks of North Carolina. Cyndi was born in 1959 in Martinsville, Indiana, to a young Army pilot and his wife. Her travels began at the age of three months when her father was stationed in Germany in the early 1960s. A proud Army brat, Cyndi moved frequently from one army base to another as her father's military career advanced. In 1970, the family moved to Bangkok, Thailand, where they lived and traveled for two years. Her military upbringing has left her with a lifelong passion for travel and an appreciation of a variety of artistic and cultural expressions. In her adult years, Cyndi has continued traveling extensively around the world. A three-week photographic safari in Kenya also helped shape her artistic vision and deepened her commitment to wildlife preservation around the globe.

A 1981 graduate of the University of Virginia, Cyndi holds a bachelor's degree in religion and psychology. She also earned a master's degree from George Washington University in administrative sciences. Cyndi taught computer programming and applications at a community college in Virginia before making the decision to be a stay-at-home mother to her two sons, Ryan and Austin.

In 2012, just as Cyndi was entering her empty nest years, her life took a sudden and unexpected turn—a turn that ultimately led her to pursue her dream of being a professional artist. Taking on the moniker "CJ Newlife," Cyndi devoted herself to learning all she could about the art of photography and soon found herself on a spiritual and physical journey with her camera as her constant companion. She began selling her work at art shows, festivals, and galleries in North Carolina and Virginia. Cyndi is now a member of Nikon Professional Services, the Chesapeake Bay Art Association, the Carolina Nature Photographers Association, the Dare County Arts Council, the Kill Devil Hills Cooperative Gallery, and the National Association of Independent Artists.

While Cyndi enjoys shooting a wide range of subjects, her largest and most treasured body of work centers around the ancient Japanese concept of wabi-sabi. Cyndi has spent the last five years searching for images that in her opinion define the concept, exploring small forgotten towns in the Southeastern United States as well as exotic locations in Costa Rica and most recently Thailand. Cyndi's lifelong dream of returning to her childhood home in Bangkok finally came true. She was thrilled to revisit and photograph the interesting places and subjects that left an indelible impression on her as a child and that planted the seeds of her future passion for all things wabi-sabi. Cyndi's wabi-sabi project can be seen on her website wabisabiimages.com.

Much of Cyndi's recent work focuses on the natural beauty of the Outer Banks, from the ocean waters to the abundant wildlife that inhabits this remote region of North Carolina. This body of work can be seen on the website obxbeachscapes.com.

You can learn more about Cyndi and view all of her work at the website cjnewlifephotography.com. CJ Newlife Photography can also be found on Facebook and Instagram.

Contact:
cjnewlife12@gmail.com
PO Box 3068, Kill Devil Hills, NC 27948
cjnewlifephotography.com